Contents

Introduction

I have painted everything in this book on an oriental theme by interpreting the designs on antique porcelain. All the pieces faithfully reproduce the spirit of the historic designs and the colours used by early masters of the art of painting on porcelain.

You can paint flowers, birds, butterflies, deer, dragons and phoenixes in an infinite variety of combinations, choosing the composition, colours and style to suit yourself. Each design is shown in detail, almost step by step, from the pencil sketch to the different stages of painting.

The designs are all painted on white porcelain: the choice of object is up to you. The motifs can be adapted for use on all sorts of white porcelain objects, such as vases, bowls, plates, sweet-dishes, ash-trays, tea caddies, cache-pots, platters, etc. All these are suitable for the designs in this book.

The motifs will also appeal to artists in other media – for painting on wood, or even on silk or other fabrics.

Painting on Porcelain

Oriental designs

The author would like to thank her husband for taking all the photographs in this book and Laurence Noirot for helping to correct the manuscript.

Painting on Porcelain

Oriental designs

ANNICK PERRET

SEARCH PRESS

First published in Great Britain 1995

Search Press Limited
Wellwood, North Farm Road,
Tunbridge Wells, Kent TN2 3DR

First published in French by Dessain et Tolra, Paris, in
1994, under the title of *Peinture sur Porcelaine: Motifs
d'Extrême-Orient*. Copyright © 1994 Dessain et Tolra.
Photography by Claude Perret.

English translation © 1995 Search Press Ltd.

If you have any diffficulty in obtaining the materials
mentioned in this book, please contact the Publishers,
Search Press, at the address above for assistance.

There are references to sable brushes in this book.
It is the Publishers' custom to recommend synthetic
materials as substitutes for animal products
wherever possible: many brushes made from
artificial fibres will be found to be as satisfactory as
brushes made of natural fibres.

ISBN 0 85532 786 3

Printed in Malaysia

History

The art of ceramics is a very ancient one. The first potteries appeared around 7000BC, more or less across the whole world. Ceramics were quite highly advanced even in prehistoric times.

In China, the evolution of ceramics culminated in the invention, under the Tang dynasty (618 to 907), of porcelain, which combined the three essential qualities of hardness, resonance and translucency. The Chinese used a feldspar clay called *kao-ling* ('bone of porcelain') with the addition of a powdered white stone called *po-fouetseu* ('flesh of porcelain'). Fusing these two elements at a temperature of around 1450°C (2642°F) resulted in porcelain.

Chinese porcelain

Chinese motifs form a sort of language, each one having a symbolic meaning. The main source of inspiration is nature, especially flowers. The following flowers evoke the four seasons.

Spring: the peony, emblem of wealth, good fortune and good breeding.

Summer: the lotus, regarded by Buddhists as a symbol of purity of heart.

Autumn: the chrysanthemum, symbolising melancholy.

Winter: cherry blossom, symbolising longevity.

Bamboo represents firmness and uprightness; while the butterfly is the emblem of married happiness, joy and longevity, and also represents summer. The deer is the symbol of grace and also of honour; the tiger, king of wild beasts, symbolises energy and appears in the Chinese calendar in the month of January. The magpie stands for *joie de vivre*.

The dragon has many meanings. It symbolises the sky and spring. Painted with five claws, it represents the emperor; when it is shown with a ball, the ball symbolises the pearl of power, which the dragon is thought to have been searching for. A blue dragon represents the East.

The phoenix, emblem of the Empress of China, symbolises beauty and also stands for summer. Its feathers of four colours got their names from the four points of the compass.

The reason there is such a wide variety of painted porcelain is that the national styles diversified over the course of the centuries under the different dynasties, and then the styles were adapted to suit foreign tastes on porcelain made specifically for export.

I am not going to go into the history of Chinese porcelain in any detail, fascinating though it is, but here are a few of the most important periods, starting from the period of the Five Dynasties.

Under the Song dynasty (960–1280) ceramics were very popular. The work was so good that the imperial factories had to multiply to keep pace with demand and to ensure sufficient supply for export, especially to the countries of Asia.

Under the Yuan dynasty (1280–1368) the exquisite 'blue and white' porcelain appeared: cobalt blue on a fine white porcelain body, coated with a clear glaze. Under the long Ming dynasty (1368–1644) the very finest blue and white work was produced, and there was a general renaissance of the art of ceramics. Production was centralised at Jingdezhen, in the Imperial factory, which became, over the centuries, the main producer of porcelain in the world.

At the same time, porcelain in two colours, then five, was being produced. This was known in Europe as *famille verte* and *famille rose*, terms that first began to be used in the nineteenth century.

In 1712 there were more than 20,000 families of potters in Jingdezhen. From the seventeenth to the eighteenth century, Chinese ceramics conquered the West and introduced the taste for chinoiserie. At the same time, Chinese porcelain lost its originality and freedom by adapting to foreign taste and becoming mass-produced.

Japanese porcelain – the Kakiemon style

Proof of the inventiveness of Japanese potters exists from neolithic times, but above all it was the influence of China, beginning in the third century BC, that stamped Japanese pottery.

It was the Zen tea ceremony that really developed the pottery industry in Japan, towards the middle of the sixteenth century. After the end of that century the term *raku*, meaning 'pleasure in leisure', or 'enjoyment', came to be applied to Japanese pottery. The name is still used for one of the characteristic techniques of Japanese ceramics to this day.

The discovery of kaolin in the seventeenth century marked the start of Japanese porcelain-making. Many pieces were copied from Chinese porcelain, especially the 'blue and white' ware. From the second half of the seventeenth century the Japanese were rivals with the Chinese for the European market via the East India Company.

The Kakiemon style gets its name from its inventor, Sakaida Kizaemon (1596–1666), known as Kakiemon, who founded a factory which is still owned by his family today. His name is associated with the birth of Japanese porcelain and with coloured on-glaze designs with which he experimented after buying the secrets of enamelling from the Chinese. His efforts were crowned with success around 1646. His descendants took up his style again, which during the eighteenth century influenced some European producers of porcelain, especially Meissen and Chantilly.

The most frequently used motifs are bamboo; twisted pine-trunks; flowery hedges; chrysanthemums and rocks; mythical birds in lively colours; tigers and bamboo thickets; and quails.

A great part of Kakiemon's production was first bought by the Dutch, who then began to make imitations adapted to European taste, and then by the

whole of Europe. The main characteristic of the Kakiemon style is the way the white porcelain background is allowed to show through the light design.

As soon as they saw that Japanese designs were appreciated in Europe, the Chinese started to imitate them, just as certain European manufacturers were doing.

The East India Company

From the end of the sixteenth century, the development of commerce with the countries of the Far East by Western companies assured the import of Chinese porcelain, especially the *famille rose* dinner services, which were much sought after.

The establishment of the East India companies – English in 1600, Dutch in 1602, and French in 1604 – meant that large quantities of porcelain were imported into Europe and sold at auction as each ship arrived.

Rich Europeans sent models of designs to China to be copied; the Chinese, marvellous copyists, reproduced them. All the grandest families had dinner services made with their coats of arms on; after Madame de Pompadour, provincial nobility followed the trend. And so Chinese porcelain became very popular.

Later, under Louis XVI, imports of oriental porcelain into France slowed because the factories of Sèvres and Limoges were making their own chinoiserie designs: in 1769 kaolin was discovered near Limoges, which meant that hard-paste porcelain could be made.

From the eighteenth century onwards, European makers of porcelain and earthenware in Delft, Nevers, Rouen, Saint-Cloud, Mennecy, Chantilly and Meissen began to produce Chinese designs in order to set themselves up in competition to Chinese imports.

A vessel of the East India Company at sea – eighteenth century (polychromatic decoration painted in red of iron and grey).

Meissen

The first hard porcelain was made at Meissen, in Saxony, in 1709, after kaolin was discovered in Europe by the physicist Böttger. The factory at Meissen, of which he became director, was created in 1710 and kept its manufacturing secret until 1718, when a rival set up in Vienna and was quickly followed by others.

France had to wait until 1751 to make its first hard porcelain, from kaolin imported from Germany.

The influence of Far-Eastern porcelain was very important at Meissen. In fact, August II the Strong, Elector of Saxony and King of Poland, had a considerable collection of Chinese and Japanese pieces which the porcelain painters of Meissen used as models – especially the Chinese *famille verte* style and the Indian flowers in the style of Kakiemon. After the Elector's death, the range widened: figurines, statuettes and graceful knick-knacks spread the taste for the rocaille style across Europe.

Delft

In the seventeenth and eighteenth centuries, Delft was the most important earthenware-producing centre in Europe, with studios dedicated to painting and imitating Far-Eastern porcelain forwarded by the Dutch East India Company.

In the middle of the seventeenth century, Abraham de Cooge was the greatest master of the Delft school and the art of ceramics in general. His work ceased to be simple copying and moved on to a free interpretation of Western motifs; its introduction into France in the seventeenth century and the first half of the eighteenth was very important.

The factories of Delft served as models for those that opened in France under Louis XIV and produced the porcelain known as 'Dutch porcelain'.

Colours

Colours

Porcelain painting has the soft, transparent look of a watercolour. However, to paint on porcelain you will need special colours for what is called 'soft firing': the designs are painted on ordinary white glazed porcelain or china using vitrifying colours. I use various makes of powder colours: these are metal-oxide colourings which, when they are mixed with flux, adhere to the glaze.

Test colour palette

Before painting an actual porcelain object, make a test colour palette. I have painted one on page 12, using a 20 x 20cm (8 x 8in) tile, to demonstrate the colours used to paint the motifs in this book. It is always useful to do your own tests, but it is helpful to know that some colours can be mixed and others cannot (reds and yellows, for example).

Preparing colours

To make up colours for freehand painting with a brush, grind up the powder on a very clean white earthenware tile using a small steel palette knife and mix it to a smooth paste with a few drops of rectified turpentine essence, fat oil and carnation oil or oil of spike lavender (or aspic or cloves). (Alternatively, use a ready-made medium consisting of a mixture of these oils, replacing the traditional preparation.)

To make up colours to use with a steel-nibbed pen, follow the same procedure as above but make it much more liquid by adding more rectified turpentine essence. This technique lets you get some very fine details in your work but does need some experience. I fix the contours by a cool firing (about 50°C (122°F)) before painting in the colours. There are other ways of working with a pen, but I prefer this one, which gives me a more flexible outline.

You can prepare the colours in advance if you like, putting them in little china pots and writing their names on the lids. Then place them in a sealed metal box to keep the dust out of them and they will be all right for up to a week. When you come to use them, just put them on the earthenware tile and work them well with a little rectified turpentine essence.

For drawing with fat oil, using a steel-nibbed pen, prepare the colour using fat oil and turpentine or a mixture of petrol and fat oil (it must be very fluid). (This drawing needs a first firing before you carry on working, but looks very delicate and graceful.)

Preparing porcelain for painting

Before you start, clean your porcelain thoroughly with a cloth dipped in white spirit to remove all grease.

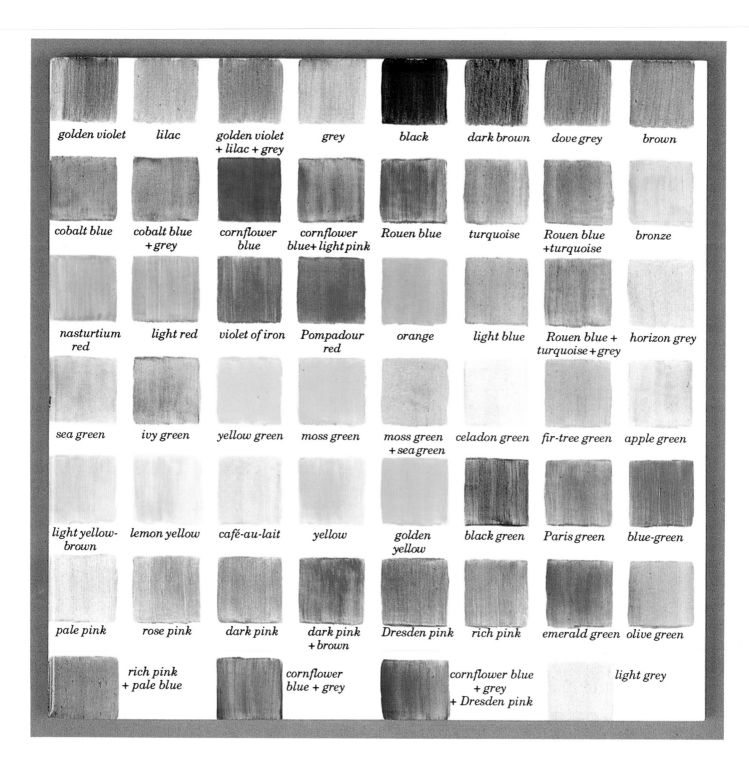

golden violet	lilac	golden violet + lilac + grey	grey	black	dark brown	dove grey	brown
cobalt blue	cobalt blue + grey	cornflower blue	cornflower blue + light pink	Rouen blue	turquoise	Rouen blue + turquoise	bronze
nasturtium red	light red	violet of iron	Pompadour red	orange	light blue	Rouen blue + turquoise + grey	horizon grey
sea green	ivy green	yellow green	moss green	moss green + sea green	celadon green	fir-tree green	apple green
light yellow-brown	lemon yellow	café-au-lait	yellow	golden yellow	black green	Paris green	blue-green
pale pink	rose pink	dark pink	dark pink + brown	Dresden pink	rich pink	emerald green	olive green
	rich pink + pale blue		cornflower blue + grey		cornflower blue + grey + Dresden pink		light grey

Materials and equipment

Brushes

I use a selection of high-quality sable paintbrushes of different sizes.

Brushes for outlining. Brushes for outlining and shading should be very fine to enable you to paint all the little details you will need.

Pointers. Not so fine as those above, these are used for general painting.

Medium brushes. These are useful for spreading background colour.

Stippler brushes. Use these for filling in small areas.

Cut liners. These have long, sloping hairs and are used for painting lines and bands with the aid of a turntable.

To look after your brushes and foam pads, clean them with turpentine and then wash them carefully with water and household soap.

Carnation oil, oil of spike lavender, oil of aspic

These prolong the time a prepared colour is workable and stop it drying too fast. Carnation oil dries less quickly than the others.

Fat oil

Fat oil is thickened turpentine essence which is used to prepare colours.

Fibreglass brush

This is a special fibreglass brush for burnishing gold.

Flux

This is a mixture of silicaceous sand which helps the colourings adhere to the porcelain and forms a glaze. It comes as a white powder which you mix with a colour to cover a large area in order to get a lovely high-gloss surface after firing.

Gold

For delicate gold highlights, use matt gold (a black liquid consisting of 24 to 32 per cent fine gold) and polish it after firing with an agate burnisher, a damp sable brush, or a special fibreglass brush. You will need a gold diluting liquid, several brushes to be kept solely for using with matt gold, and a glass rod for stirring the gold well before use. Bright gold, which has a low gold content (12 per cent), shines after firing.

Iridescent lustre

Lustres are metallic colouring salts. Iridescent lustre will give you mother-of-pearl effects on butterflies' wings (see the square Chinese-style ashtray on page 93). Clean the brush, which you should keep just for using with lustres, with a solvent.

Materials and equipment for painting on porcelain.

Masking fluid

You can also get some good effects with masking fluid, which you use to cover up parts of a design which you do not wish to be coloured when you are painting a background. It is a special red or blue substance used to protect a part of a design which is to stay white. Paint the fluid on and let it dry, then brush or pad on the coloured background over the whole surface, let the colour dry, and then peel off the masking fluid. It comes off easily. Do not forget to remove it before firing! Clean the brush used to apply it with white spirit.

Muffle kiln

A ceramic kiln with a muffle is used for soft-firing on-glaze decorations on porcelain. If you do not want to invest in a hobby ceramic kiln, get your work fired by a specialist shop or studio. An enamel kiln can be used for firing very small pieces of porcelain.

Palette knives

You will need these knives with flexible steel blades for preparing your colours.

Solvent

Use solvent for cleaning brushes you have used for gold and lustres.

Special pencil

You will need to buy a special lithographic pencil for drawing on porcelain. The line it makes disappears in firing.

Steel-nibbed pen

I use a pen-holder with a steel nib for drawing fine outlines and details.

White spirit

This is used to degrease porcelain before you draw and paint on it, and to clean brushes used for gold and lustre. A mineral solvent somewhere between petrol and paraffin, it has replaced turpentine as a paint-thinner.

Techniques

Far-Eastern designs are fresh, light and fluid; the style of drawing, very stylised, can be enriched by contrasting colourings. The flowers look geometric and there are no effects of light and shade.

There are plenty of models by the great masters which you can interpret, once you have some technical knowledge. In fact, practising copying from models is a good way to start: you can soon get a feeling for colours and composition. After that, you can start taking liberties!

There are many techniques. I shall simply describe the way I paint, which is a common technique. My aim is to help any artist, whether beginner or more advanced, to paint these marvellous designs, which come from a variety of museums.

First I painted them in watercolour, and then I painted them on the porcelain objects, adding my own personal touch at the same time.

Banding

Banding or threading is done with a turntable (also known as a banding wheel or whirler) – a circular platform which rotates. Hold your outliner brush with a steady hand and touch the porcelain item lightly with it while the turntable is going round to get an even band of colour or gold.

Firing

I build up the painted design over the course of several firings (between two and five firings at different temperatures), according to the difficulty of the motif, the size of the piece of porcelain and the degree of finish of the gold. Remember to keep the kiln at a medium temperature – 780–820°C (1436–1508°F) – for at least ten minutes to give a glossy lustre to the colours. Nasturtium red and light red should be fired at between 700 and 750°C (1292 and 1382°F).

Note: if you want a matt effect, you will have to fire at a lower temperature – around 650°C (1202°F). (See the *Heron* design on pages 44–45).

You should always fire gold last of all, after all the painted colours have been fired. You will need to fire at 800°C (1472°F) when the gold is directly on the white porcelain and at 660°C (1220°F) when it is on a coloured background.

Some designs begin with an outline drawn with a pen or a small, fine-pointed brush – fix this with an intermediate firing as described above before applying the colours. To get a lovely transparent effect, apply the colours successively in several firings. Some will need their details touching up between each firing.

I have given you some technical advice and the number of firings you will need with each design in this book.

Painting a background

You can paint a coloured background by mixing the colours with medium (seee page 11) and then 'padding' it with a foam pad (get several sizes of these). I always add a little flux to my chosen colour to give the porcelain more luminosity.

Pouncing

You can draw your design freehand straight on to the glaze of your chosen porcelain object, or you can use a tracing. If you are doing a series of objects – say, plates – you can use a pounced pattern to repeat the motif. Draw the design on tracing paper and prick the outline with a needle, making small, regular holes. Then turn the paper over and rub it gently with fine glasspaper (to open out the holes). Rub the pouncer (a cloth pad containing or impregnated with pounce – powdered charcoal) across the tracing in a swishing motion and the charcoal will mark the outline.

Relief

For some Chinese or Indian-flower designs you can use the old technique of relief, which uses a mixture of Chinese white or white enamel for part of the design, and other colours, mixed with fat oil and rectified turpentine essence, for the other part. This will give a design more contrast and make it appear in low relief.

Note: This technique should be used with care, especially when firing, which should be carried out gently to stop the relief coming off the enamel. In this book I have not used the technique, from personal taste; to get contrasts I have gone over the colours again (or part of them) between each firing.

Scraping

This decorative technique involves scratching the colour when dry with a scraper/rubbing-out knife, toothpick or small wooden stick to produce white designs and patterns in the background.

Designs

Flowers and tendrils

This Chinese-style design is painted on a jardinière 22.5cm (9in) high and 20cm (8in) in diameter. The flowers and curling tendrils surround the character *cheou* (meaning longevity). A frieze of *jou-y* (meaning 'according to your desire') motifs can be painted round the top of the jardinière.

Colours
Rouen blue or cobalt blue, or cornflower blue mixed with light grey.

Firing
Four firings on porcelain (the last one should be at 820°C (1508°F).

First firing: take the design over the entire surface of the jardinière. Paint the contours in blue using a small brush.

Second firing: add the friezes. Paint the inside of the flower petals with diluted colour.

Third firing: accentuate the flowers in dark blue. Add a light touch of pale blue to the tendrils for 'flames'. Paint the bands using a turntable or banding wheel.

Fourth firing: touch up the colours. Pad a pale-blue background on the top and bottom of the jardinière, on the friezes.

18

Floral design with gold highlights

This floral design decorates a lidded vase 35cm (14in) high. You could paint it in a variety of alternative colours: Dresden pink and gold; dark brown and gold; Pompadour red and gold; olive green and gold...

Colours

Rouen blue or cornflower blue mixed with grey; 32 per cent matt gold.

Firing

Three firings at 800–820°C (1472–1508°F).

First firing: draw the design all round the vase using a special pencil for drawing on porcelain. Outline the contours with a small fine-pointed brush and Rouen blue or your mixture of cornflower blue and grey.

Second firing: paint the interior of the flowers and leaves, and paint the base of the vase using a thick brush. The colour has to be diluted (leave a narrow white border close to the outlines). Even it out with a stippler brush if necessary. Now paint the knob of the lid and the broad bands of matt gold.

Third firing: paint a second coat of Rouen blue inside the flowers and leaves, as shown, and inside the stylised rocks at the base, without completely filling the motifs. Add the gold highlights and touch up the bands.

Oriental flowers

There is an Islamic feel to this floral design in blue on a gold background. It would probably look best painted on a decorative plate or a round sweet-dish.

Colours
Cornflower blue, bright gold (for the background), 32 per cent matt gold.

Firing
Four firings at around 800°C (1472°F).

First firing: draw the motif on your chosen piece of porcelain. Paint the outlines in blue with a fine brush, plus the flowers and stems. Model the leaves with a broader pointed brush.

Second firing: paint a background of matt gold, or use bright gold, which is cheaper.

Third firing: dilute the colour and paint the paler flowers. Apply a second coat of gold (32 per cent matt gold).

Fourth firing: touch up the blue with darker tones.

Blue peacock

This oriental motif, inspired by the Delft style (around 1712), would look good on a platter, an oval box or an octagonal plate.

Colours
Three shades of blue: blue-black, cornflower blue, and light blue. Make the blue-black yourself by mixing cornflower blue with a touch of black.

Firing
Three firings at 800–820°C (1472–1508°F).

First firing: draw part of the design with a steel-nibbed pen using blue-black. Sketch the leaves with a brush using cornflower blue, and then, on the flat rim of the plate, paint a border of blue scales.

Second firing: paint the flowers and rocks in light blue and the peacock in blue-black, cornflower blue and pale blue.

Third firing: accentuate the colours.

Flowers and Chinese butterfly with touches of gold

This Chinese-style vase, which is 23cm (9in) high, shows off the blue design on a textured background with touches of gold.

Colours

Cobalt blue mixed with a touch of black, or cornflower blue mixed with grey, or Rouen blue. Use flux for the background.

Firing

Four firings at 800–820°C (1472–1508°F).

First firing: draw the motif and paint it as you did on page 20 (I have used cobalt blue with a touch of black).

Second firing: cover the design with masking fluid and paint a background with your foam pad. Use the same cobalt blue but add a little flux to it. When it has dried slightly, scratch out the patterns with a small pointed stick or toothpick.

Third firing: touch up the colour on the flowers and leaves. Paint the bands using a turntable.

Fourth firing: add the small golden highlights to the design.

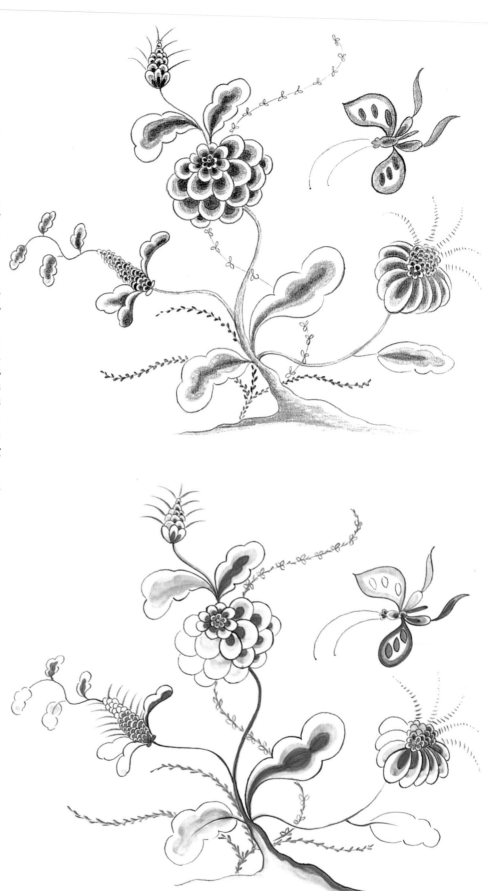

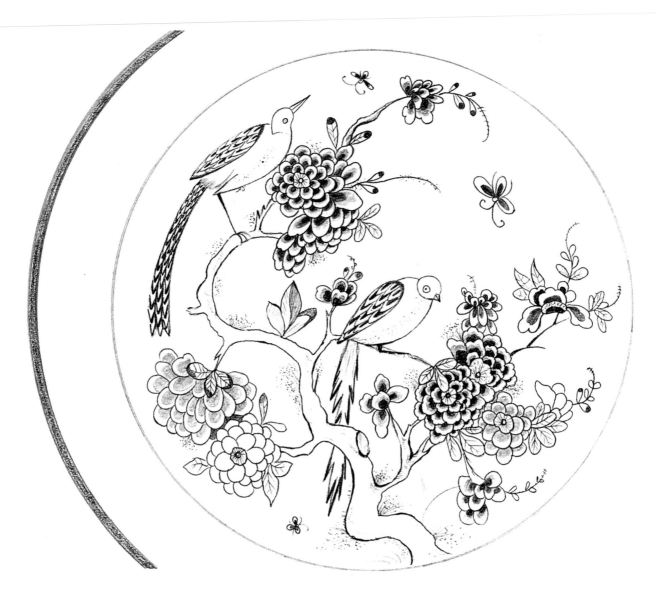

Birds on flowering branches

This design, inspired by the Delft style, is suitable for a plate or vase. The four-sided vase I have used is 37cm (14½in) tall.

Colours
Rouen blue, 32 per cent matt gold.

Firing
Four or five firings (the fifth for touching up if necessary) at 800–820°C (1472–1508°F).

Sketch the birds and branches with a brush using Rouen blue and draw in the outlines of the flowers and butterflies with a steel-nibbed pen.

Pad a light background on the handles, which you will highlight with gold. The base of the vase is made up of tiny blue spirals done with a pen.

Finally, add the gold bands.

Note: you will get a medium tone by putting two coats of the same colour on top of one another, with a firing in between.

Flowers and leaves on a graduated background

I have painted this motif on a vase shaped like a double gourd. It is 26cm (10¼in) high.

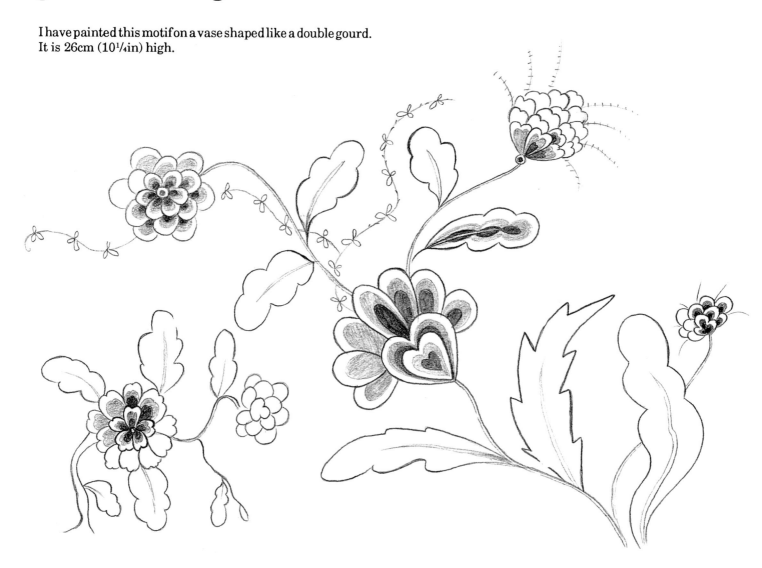

Colours
Rouen blue (add some flux for the background), matt gold.

Firing
Four firings at 800–820°C (1472–1508°F).

First firing: sketch the design and add the outlines in blue, using a brush.

Second firing: add a shaded background, using masking fluid to cover the design while you do so.

Third firing: paint the insides of the flowers and leaves with diluted colour.

Fourth firing: work on the motifs again with a darker colour to get some depth. Paint a band of matt gold round the base of the vase.

Lotus flowers

Here I have painted an example of a Chinese design for a flat-sided vase. Lotus flowers symbolise summer.

Colours
A mixture of Rouen blue and turquoise.

Firing
Two firings at 800°C (1472°F).

First firing: sketch the design on to the porcelain. Dilute the colour and paint the motifs (leaves, lotus flowers and birds) with a medium-sized pointed paintbrush.

Second firing: shade the motifs, touch up the outlines, and add highlights to the composition with a fine brush.

Note: you will need a third firing if you want to add a frieze in gold or accentuate the colour in a darker tone.

Mandarin ducks

This Chinese design in blue monochrome consists of a pair of Mandarin ducks (symbolising married happiness) swimming amongst lotus flowers and water plants. You could paint it on to a vase, a plate, a sweet-dish or an ashtray.

Colours
Rouen blue or cornflower blue mixed with a little grey.

Firing
Two or three firings at 800–820°C (1472–1508°F).

First firing: sketch the design on to the porcelain, then outline the lotus flowers and ducks using a fine brush. Paint the leaves, stems and water with a broader brush.

Second firing: add the palest blue to the ducks and lotus flowers. Shade the leaves with a fine brush and add the little dots along the stalks.

Third firing: if necessary, touch up the blue and accentuate the colour of the ducks and flowers with dark tones.

Two Chinese dragons

This 31.5cm (12½in) vase is decorated with two blue dragons in the Ming style, surrounded by clouds and fighting over a ball of flame marked by a spiral, symbolising thunder. The dragon's head is adorned with a few touches of gold.

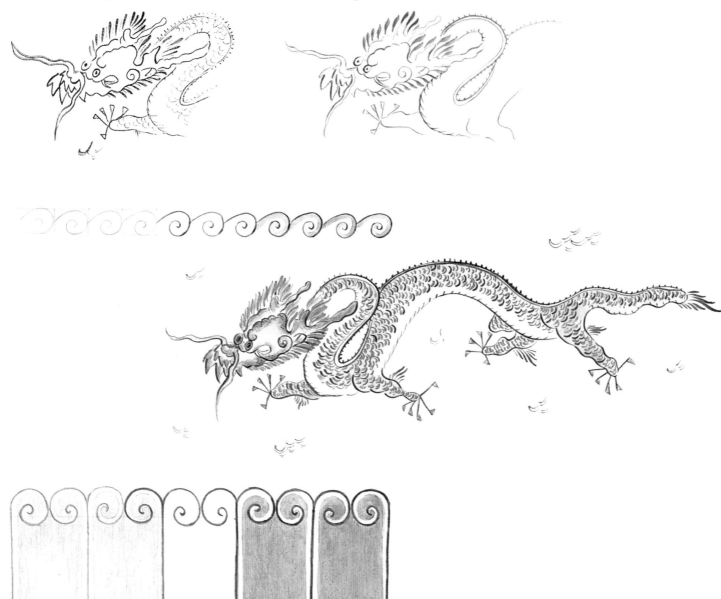

Colours
Cobalt blue with a touch of black or dark grey, matt gold, and flux (for the background).

Firing
Three firings at 800–820°C (1472–1508°F).

First firing: draw or otherwise transfer the dragon designs on to the porcelain and outline them with a small fine brush.

Second firing: paint the friezes on the body of the vase and on its base, and add the blue bands. Touch up the bodies of the dragons with diluted background colour.

Third firing: highlight the scales and heads of the dragons with gold. Pad a background on the frieze at the base of the vase, either using masking fluid or scraping off the colour to leave a line of white along the verticals of the frieze pattern. Paint a thin gold band around the neck of the vase.

Landscape with deer

This blue-and-white motif was inspired by a Chinese 'deer' design from the Kangzi and Kian-long era.

Colours
Rouen blue, matt gold.

Firing
Two firings at 800°C (1472°F).

First firing: draw the design on to a plate. Using a brush and a steel-nibbed pen, paint the deer and part of the composition with diluted colour.

Second firing: go over the blue again. Use matt gold for the rim of the plate.

Note: if your plate has a wide rim, draw a stylised floral motif round it (see the sketch) and paint it as you did on page 28.

Blue and green design with birds

This composition is done in two colours, green and blue, with lightly shaded foliage. Inspired by the Delft style, it is painted here on a 35cm (14in) tall Chinese-style vase with a lid.

Colours
Cornflower blue, moss green, violet of iron.

Firing
Three firings at 800°C (1472°F).

First firing: sketch the design. Paint the birds, the branches, and the tree-trunk in blue. Then paint the leaves in moss green, using a medium-sized paintbrush, and outline the flowers in blue, using a very fine brush.

Second firing: colour the inside of the flowers with diluted cornflower blue and paint the friezes.

Third firing: go over the flowers again (the darker parts). Touch up the birds, the branches, and the tree-trunk. Shade the leaves with a mixture of moss green and violet of iron. Finally, add the blue bands using a turntable.

38

Blue birds on a yellow background

'Yellow and blue' Chinese porcelain was first produced during the reign of Xuande. Yellow, the imperial colour, was used as a background for motifs painted in blue. I have taken this bird motif from the reign of Yong-cheng (1723–35) in the Qing period. The vase is 30cm (12in) high.

Colours

Golden yellow, Rouen blue, flux (for the background).

Firing

Three firings at 800°C (1472°F).

First firing: draw the design all round the lidded vase. Using a medium-sized broad brush, paint the birds and bamboo branches. Add the bands using a turntable.

Second firing: mix the yellow with one-third of flux, prepared with medium. Put masking fluid all over the blue design and allow it to dry. Now apply the yellow background with a large synthetic foam pad, making sure that it is even. After the yellow has dried, remove the masking fluid before firing.

Third firing: shade and touch up the whole of the blue design.

Ducks and lotus flowers on a maize-yellow background

This design was inspired by Chinese tapestry. The vase is 26cm (10¼in) high.

Colours

Dark rose pink, light rose pink, brownish violet of iron, nasturtium red, cornflower blue, light blue, blue-black, maize yellow, green-black, yellow, emerald green, ivy green, grey, flux (for the background), matt gold.

Firing

Four firings at 780–800°C (1436–1472°F).

First firing: draw the design on to the vase. With a fine brush, outline some of the waterlilies with dark rose pink (the inside of the petals will be painted pale pink) and the lotus flowers with nasturtium red mixed with violet of iron (the inside will be painted gold in a subsequent firing). With a large brush, paint the duck using pale blue, yellow, blue-black and nasturtium red. Indicate the water with blue, then the foliage, giving it a sense of light and shade by using dark and light greens. Scratch out the veins in the large waterlily leaf with a toothpick.

Second firing: cover the painted motifs with masking fluid and allow it to dry. Now add a background (prepare a maize-yellow or light yellow-brown colour with medium and some flux) using a large foam pad. Remove the masking fluid before firing. For the neck of the vase, scratch out a patterned frieze with a toothpick.

Third firing: accentuate the foliage with emerald green mixed with black-green. Shade the ducks with a stronger version of the colours you used to sketch them. On the waterlilies which you outlined in nasturtium red and violet of iron, add matt gold to the petals. Paint the fine bands of matt gold at the top and bottom of the vase and highlight the frieze on the neck of the vase with matt gold.

Fourth firing: touch up the colours and the gold.

Heron, flowers and leaves

This multi-coloured design with gold on a celadon-green background has a Chinese influence. Here it is applied to a six-sided vase 30cm (12in) high.

Colours
Celadon green, flux, ivy green, fir-tree green, rose pink, light pink, light grey, medium grey, black, nasturtium red, bronze.

Firing
Five firings.

First firing: trace or copy the heron design on to three alternate sides of the vase, and the stylised lotus flowers on to the other three sides. Using a large brush, paint the leaves, partly in dark ivy green and partly in diluted fir-tree green. Outline the flowers in rose pink with a fine brush and paint the inside of the petals in light pink with a medium-sized brush. Sketch the heron in light and medium grey and black. Paint its crest nasturtium red, and its beak and claws bronze. Fire at 800°C (1472°F).

Second firing: cover all the motifs with masking fluid and pad in the celadon-green background with a large piece of foam. Do not use flux this time – the background will stay matt. The colour is prepared with fat oil. Fire at about 650°C (1202°F).

Third firing: pad a second coat of celadon green on the three sides that have the lotus flowers and on the base of the vase: this time add flux (to give a shine) and mix the colour with medium. When the colour has dried slightly, scratch little spirals all over it with a toothpick. Fire at 750°C (1382°F).

Fourth firing: touch up the colours (darken the leaves) and shade the herons. Fire at 750°C (1382°F).

Fifth firing: add the matt gold bands at the base of the vase, and outline the leaves and the hearts of the flowers with gold. You should fire gold that is on a coloured background at a temperature of between 650 and 680°C (1202 and 1256°F).

44

Composition on a pink background

This *famille rose* Chinese design is in the style of Graviata in the Kien-long period (1736–95). The four-sided vase is 30cm (12in) high.

Colours

Yellow-green, dark pink, yellow, light grey, light rose pink, horizon grey, rose pink mixed with flux (for the background), outline violet (make it yourself by mixing black-brown, dark pink and violet of iron).

Firing

Four firings at 800°C (1472°F).

First firing: for this symmetrically decorated vase, do the geometric design and transfer it to each side of the vase. Mark the outlines with outline violet, using a fine brush or a steel-nibbed pen.

Second firing: protect the masking fluid and lay down a background of rose pink prepared with medium and flux. Make sure the background is even by using a large foam pad.

Third firing: colour in the design as shown.

Fourth firing: touch up the colour. Accentuate the outlines here and there with outline violet and a fine brush. Put in some light shading details in dark rose pink inside some of the flower petals.

Multi-coloured butterflies

This charming Chinese-style *famille rose* design is very pretty. I painted it on a plate 26cm (10¼in) in diameter.

Colours
Lemon yellow, Paris green, light red, cornflower blue, outline violet, dove grey.

Firing
Three firings at 780°C (1436°F).

First firing: draw the butterflies and little sprigs of flowers. Outline the details with outline violet and a steel-nibbed pen. When it has dried, paint in some of the diluted colours (blue, green, dove grey) with a medium-sized brush.

Second firing: paint the butterflies and small flowers with a brush. Decorate the edge of the plate with nasturtium-red dots.

Third firing: strengthen all the colours in the butterflies' wings, let them dry, then go over some of the outlines yet again with outline violet.

Note: this design could also be painted on a Chinese-style vase (right). The geometric border on the neck of the vase could be painted in colour or in matt gold.

Butterflies with red insects

This would be a good project for a plate or a round trinket-box.

Colours

Light red, golden violet, Paris green, cornflower blue, lemon yellow, dark brown.

Firing

Three firings at 780°C (1436°F).

First firing: paint the outlines of the butterflies in dark brown, using a small brush, except for the butterfly with golden-violet wings, which should be outlined with its own colour. Now paint the tiny insects in red. Allow to dry, then paint in the butterflies' wings using diluted colours.

Second firing: strengthen the colours using a medium brush, and add small textural details and patterns to the wings of some of the butterflies. Shade the wings of the others.

Third firing: touch up the colours and details.

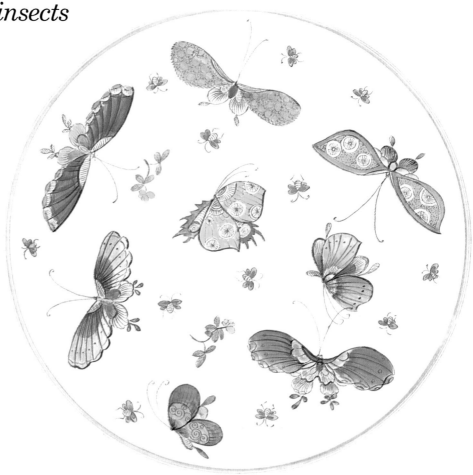

Flowers and Chinese butterflies

This would be a lovely design for a lidded vase (opposite).

Colours

Lilac, golden violet, cornflower blue, sea green, light red, moss green, black, Paris green, light golden yellow, violet of iron, dark grey.

Firing

Three firings at 780°C (1256°F).

First firing: draw the design on to the porcelain. This time you are going to do the butterflies differently – this may be a bit more difficult than outlining them and then colouring them after firing. With a fine brush and a medium-sized one, paint the butterflies' wings, then even out the colour with a very small stippling brush. Colour the flowers with lilac, water green and cornflower blue, and outline the red flowers with a steel-nibbed pen or a fine brush. Sketch in the leaves with Paris green and moss green.

Second firing: outline the butterflies with black softened with dark grey, using a fine brush, and add the fine details to the wings. Shade the leaves with violet of iron mixed with moss green. Strengthen the colour of the peony with light red.

Third firing: general touching up.

Polychromatic landscape with dragon handles

This Chinese motif, inspired by the *famille verte* period (reign of Kang-xi; 1662–1722), uses many colours but the dominant one is green. The moulded handles of the vase are transformed into dragons. This vase is 24cm (9½in) high.

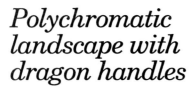

Colours
Light red, golden violet, lemon yellow, violet of iron, black, apple green, fir-tree green, moss green, ivy green, grey, brown, cornflower blue, light pink, 32 per cent matt gold.

Firing
Four or five firings at 780°C (1436°F).

First firing: draw the design on to the porcelain. With a medium-sized brush and a large one paint the birds, the foliage and the ground. Outline the flowers in light red and golden violet with a fine brush or a steel-nibbed pen, and fill in the delicate details inside the petals.

Second firing: pad the handles in grey using a piece of foam. Accentuate and darken the composition here and there.

Third firing: shade the leaves and the birds. Fill in the flowers with colour.

Fourth firing: highlight the moulded handles with matt gold. Paint a broad band of matt gold at the neck and base of the vase.

Fifth firing: if necessary, touch up the gold.

Note: this design would also be suitable for a plate.

Chinese bird

Here is a bird motif inspired by the *famille verte* style (eighteenth-century China). It would suit a round trinket-box, a plate, an ashtray, or a vase.

Colours
Nasturtium red, a mixture of grey and golden violet, sea green, ivy green, violet of iron, and a mixture of Rouen blue and turquoise.

Firing
Two firings at 750–780°C (1382–1436°F).

First firing: draw the design on to the porcelain. Paint the bird with diluted colours and a large brush, using nasturtium red, ivy green, and Rouen blue mixed with turquoise. Paint the beak with lemon yellow and violet of iron. The branch is done in pale violet of iron and light grey, while the cherry-blossom-style flowers are painted in nasturtium red.

Second firing: shade the bird's feathers with a fine brush. The rough purplish bark of the branch is detailed with a mixture of golden violet and dark grey. Shade the leaves with violet of iron and ivy green, except for the few that you paint blue.

Bird on a branch

This is another *famille verte* Chinese-style design. I have used it to decorate a tray measuring 29.5 x 21.5cm (11½ x 8½in).

Colours
Light red, a mixture of lilac and grey (for the branch), golden violet, lemon yellow, black, cornflower blue, apple green, fir-tree green, and a mixture of brownish violet of iron and fir-tree green (to shade the leaves).

Firing
Two firings at 750–780°C (1382–1436°F).

First firing: draw the motif, then sketch the bird (a sort of magpie), the foliage and the larger branches with a large brush. Outline the flowers with a pen and light red, except for the yellow flowers, which you should outline in violet of iron. Let it dry and then lay down the colour inside the petals.

Second firing: strengthen the details on the bark using a fine brush and a mixture of grey and golden violet, adding fine hatching. Go over the petals of the red and yellow flowers again, and shade the foliage. Touch up the bird with blue and black, add some shading on its back, and pick out the little details of the feathers using violet of iron and fir-tree green.

Note: I have suggested how you could use this motif on a vase (left).

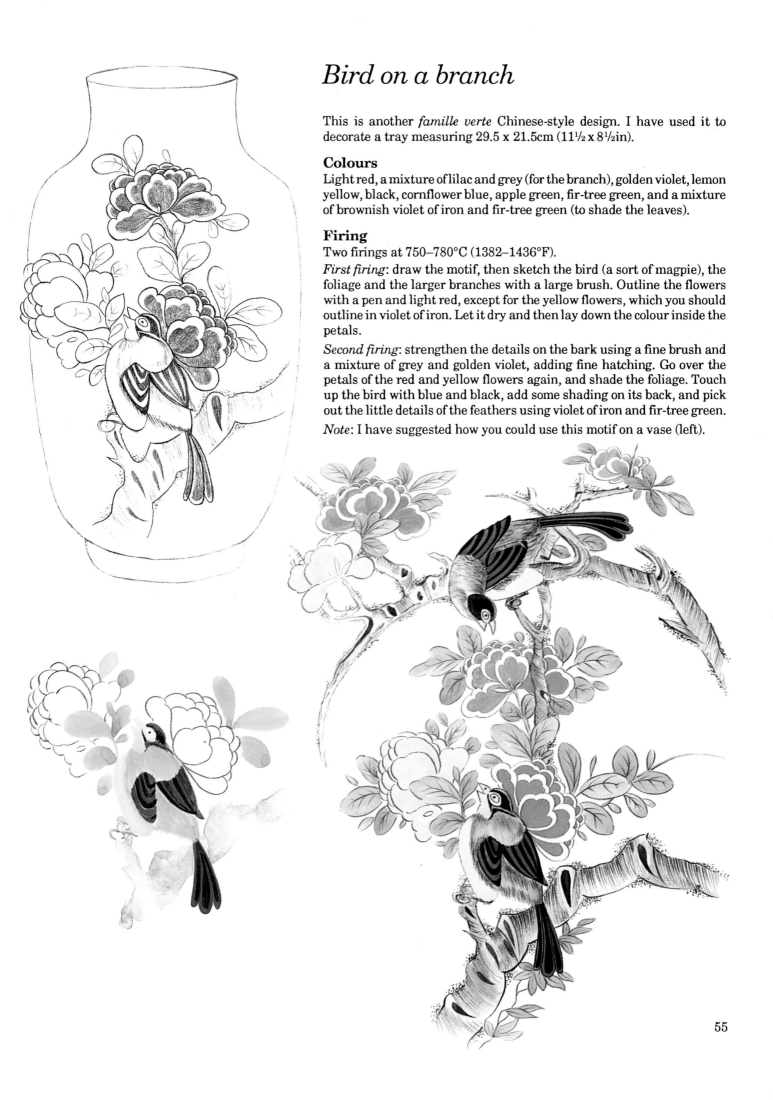

Flight of the phoenix

This is a *famille verte* Chinese design representing the flight of the finghuang (the phoenix, a mythological bird sacred to the Empress) above some peony bushes. I have painted it on a plate with a diameter of 26.5cm (10½in).

Colours

Black, a mixture of golden violet and dark grey, light red, a mixture of cobalt blue and dark grey, ivy green, a mixture of chrome sea green and moss green, lilac, matt gold.

Firing

Three firings at 750–780°C (1382–1436°F).

First firing: draw the motif on to the porcelain and outline it in red and black using a steel-nibbed pen. Sketch in the branches with light golden violet mixed with light grey, then some of the phoenix's feathers with red, ivy green and sea green.

Second firing: fill in the colours with a brush. Accentuate the details of the branches with the same colour as you used to sketch them, only stronger.

Third firing: carefully fill in the insides of the flowers with matt gold where needed, and add gold to the phoenix. Using a turntable, paint a broad band and a very fine one round the rim of the plate, using a special outliner brush which you have kept for use solely with gold.

Phoenix, stag and hind

I have painted this Chinese-style motif on a plate 26.5cm (10½in) in diameter.

Colours
Rose pink, bronze, black, Paris green, light red, cobalt blue, lemon yellow, violet of iron, black-green, 32 per cent matt gold.

Firing
Three firings at 750–780°C (1382–1436°F).

First firing: draw the design on to the porcelain. With a pen, outline the composition in black, except for those motifs which you will be painting in gold or light red. Sketch in the foliage with a brush, using Paris green, and draw the frieze in the same green round the edge of the plate, using a pen.

Second firing: colour in the design with a fine brush and a medium-sized one. Shade the stags with rose pink and bronze and paint their spots black. Using a turntable, paint a broad matt-gold band and a very fine one on the rim to outline the frieze.

Third firing: embellish the flower petals and the phoenix with matt gold, touch up the bands of gold, and accentuate any colours that need it.

Note: below I have painted a suggested alternative border for the rim of the plate.

Multi-coloured floral design

Inspired by the East India Company style (around 1740), this design is painted on a plate with an interior diameter of 23.5cm (9¼in).

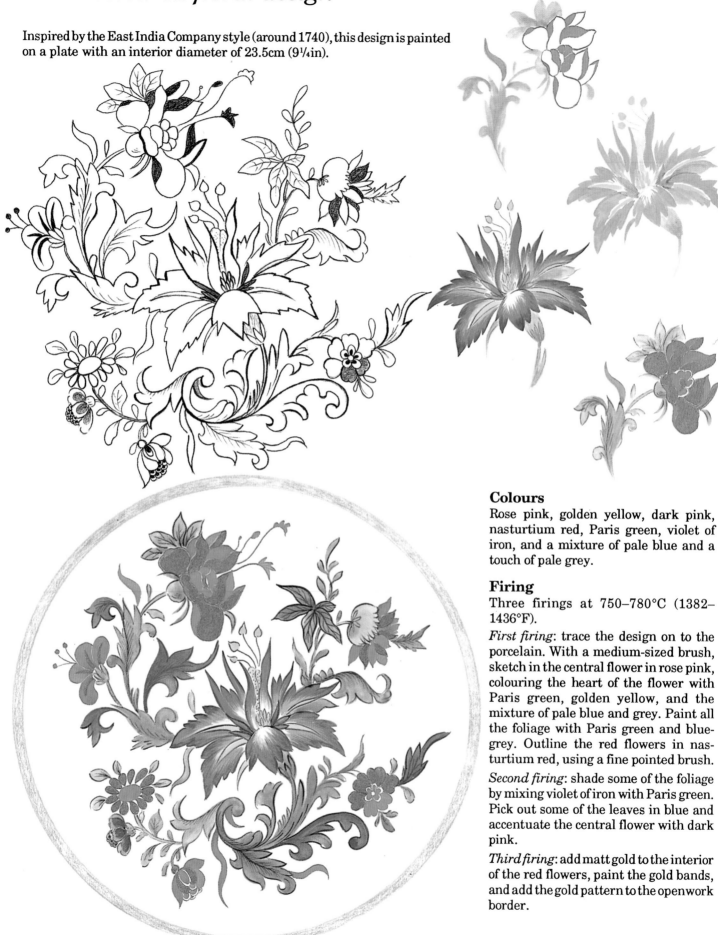

Colours

Rose pink, golden yellow, dark pink, nasturtium red, Paris green, violet of iron, and a mixture of pale blue and a touch of pale grey.

Firing

Three firings at 750–780°C (1382–1436°F).

First firing: trace the design on to the porcelain. With a medium-sized brush, sketch in the central flower in rose pink, colouring the heart of the flower with Paris green, golden yellow, and the mixture of pale blue and grey. Paint all the foliage with Paris green and blue-grey. Outline the red flowers in nasturtium red, using a fine pointed brush.

Second firing: shade some of the foliage by mixing violet of iron with Paris green. Pick out some of the leaves in blue and accentuate the central flower with dark pink.

Third firing: add matt gold to the interior of the red flowers, paint the gold bands, and add the gold pattern to the openwork border.

Petal frieze

This Chinese-inspired motif, repeated in a border, is painted on a goblet with golden handles and base. It is 16cm (6¼in) high.

Colours
Nasturtium red, black, 32 per cent matt gold.

Firing
Three firings at 750°C (1382°F).

First firing: draw three horizontal bands on the shoulder of the goblet and divide the circumference into equal segments with the aid of a tape measure. Draw the design and fill it in with nasturtium red.

Second firing: add the matt gold and paint the gold bands using a turntable. Paint the handles gold too.

Third firing: pick out the black parts of the red frieze with a fine brush. Paint a fine line using the turntable and touch up the gold on the handles.

Stylised flowers

There are masses of Chinese designs – you can borrow motifs from enamels, lacquerware, silk goods and many other sources. I have decorated this cache-pot with a stylised flower motif which I have repeated on each side. It is 16cm (6¼in) high and 14cm (5½in) in diameter.

Colours
Nasturtium red, flux (for the background), 32 per cent matt gold.

Firing
Three firings at 750°C (1382°F).

First firing: start with the red background. On each side, about half-way up, draw a semi-circle. Pad on a background of nasturtium red (mixed with flux and prepared with medium), using a foam pad.

Second firing: draw the stylised flower motifs under each semi-circle. (You can keep them even by using a tracing.) Then paint them nasturtium red. (The gold goes on at the time of the third firing.) Trace on the design on the red background and outline the motif in gold, using a brush you have kept especially for gold. Paint the feet and bands solid gold.

Third firing: now paint the outlines of the red flowers with matt gold, plus the edges of the semi-circles, and touch up the gold bands and the feet of the cache-pot.

Note: never put any gold on a decoration that you have not previously fired. The colour goes on at the time of the first firing and the matt or bright gold should be added on top of the colour at the time of the second firing.

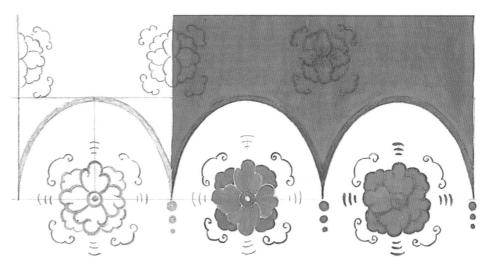

Red and gold tiger

I have painted this Meissen-style design on a 26 x 19cm (10¼ x 7½in) dish.

Colours
Nasturtium red, 32 per cent matt gold.

Firing
Three firings at 750°C (1382°F).

First firing: carefully transfer the design to the porcelain. Paint the outlines and details in nasturtium red using a fine brush.

Second firing: pad the tiger in red, shading lighter towards the head. Allow the background to dry and accentuate the details, still using red.

Third firing: using a medium-sized brush, paint the eyes and highlight the tiger's body with matt gold (see right). Paint a band of gold round the edge of the dish.

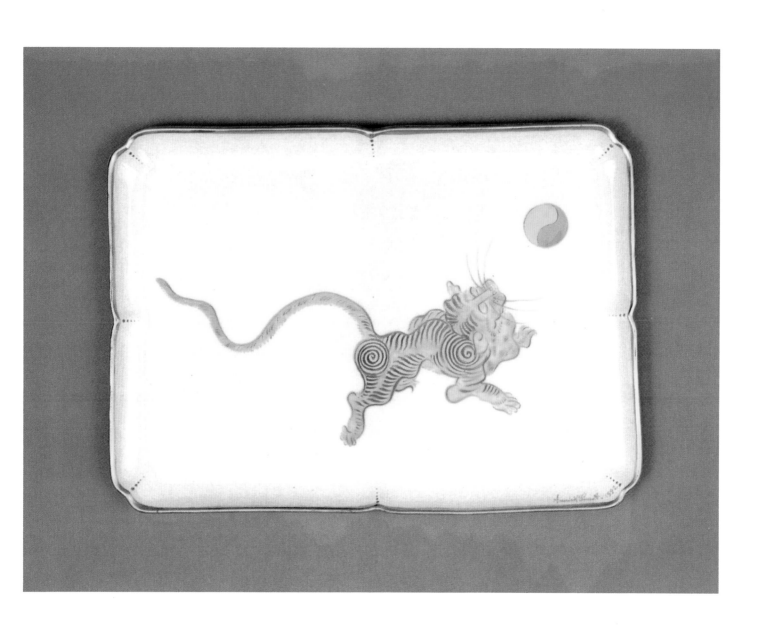

Red crane and trellis

The crane in this Meissen-style design symbolises longevity. I have painted it on a bowl 22.5 x 20cm (9 x 8in).

Colours
Nasturtium red, Paris green, sea green (for the background), a little flux, black, 32 per cent matt gold.

Firing
Three firings at 750°C (1382°F).

First firing: draw the bird on to the porcelain, outline it in nasturtium red using a fine brush, colour the beak and part of the neck, and sketch in the tail feathers with a medium-sized brush, making them a darker tone.

Second firing: paint the bird's body and feathers with diluted red and even out the colour. Pad a sea-green background round the edge of the bowl.

Third firing: add the matt gold highlights, paint a fine gold band and finish the bowl off with a delicate border of golden scales.

Fantastic creature and butterfly

This lidded vase, 35cm (14in) high, is decorated with Meissen-style motifs. The lid is embellished with a stylised floral motif.

Colours

Paris green (for the creature), light red, black, cornflower blue, golden yellow, 32 per cent matt gold.

Firing

Three firings at 750–780°C (1382–1436°F).

First firing: trace the creature on to the porcelain. With a fine brush, paint the outlines, details of the head and paws in black and the tongue in red. Outline the rest of the body in light red. Allow to dry thoroughly, then paint the tail and the animal's back with Paris green, evening out the colour.

Second firing: pad a light-red background colour on the rest of the creature's body and do its head using cornflower blue. Paint in the scales and other details on the Paris-green back.

Third firing: add touches of gold as shown on the watercolour sketch (left).

Note: I painted three bands round the neck, base and lid of the vase, using red, gold and black with a turntable.

Blue dragon-tiger

Here we have a design on a white background in the Kakiemon style (Meissen). Two sides are decorated with a stylised dahlia and the other two with the blue dragon-tiger. On the neck of this 40cm (16in) vase I have painted a butterfly which I have borrowed from *Butterflies and Indian flowers* on page 86.

Colours
Cornflower blue, golden yellow, nasturtium red, moss green, Paris green, black, matt gold.

Firing
Three firings at 750–800°C (1382–1442°F).

First firing: trace the dragon-tiger on to the vase and paint its outlines and stripes with a fine brush and some black. On the other two sides of the vase, draw a freehand dahlia twig in cornflower blue, the flowers being outlined in nasturtium red with a fine pointed brush.

Second firing: spread out the cornflower blue on the dragon-tiger's head and body, evening out the colour with a stippler brush. Paint the inside of the petals nasturtium red.

Third firing: add golden touches to some of the dahlias and accentuate any colours that need it.

Note: I have also given an alternative suggestion for using this motif on a plate (above) or on a different-shaped vase (right).

70

Phoenix on a flowery branch

This Kakiemon-style design from around 1735 comes from Chelsea, in England, where many motifs were similar to those from Meissen. The flowers look like azaleas. A golden border runs round the shoulders of the vase, while the turquoise background of the neck and lid is decorated with golden spirals.

Colours

Sea green, golden yellow, Paris green, violet of iron, light red, grey (for the bird's beak), dark brown, flux (for the background), 32 per cent matt gold.

Firing

Three firings at 750–780°C (1382–1436°F).

First firing: draw the motifs on to the different sides of the vase. With a medium-sized brush, sketch in the phoenix using golden yellow, Paris green, light red, grey, and dark brown. Paint the flower petals yellow and red, then the leaves in fir-tree green and Paris green. Spread out the background (sea green prepared with medium) with a foam pad on the top of the vase, on the lid, and on the knob of the lid. Allow to dry, then scratch out little comma-shaped marks to form a pattern, using a wooden stick or toothpick.

Second firing: with a fine brush, shade the bird and the whole of the floral composition, accentuating the little white commas with light red in places. Pick out the border in matt gold – this, in relief on the shoulders of the vase, makes a sort of collar. Finally, paint the gold bands using a turntable.

Third firing: touch up the gold if you need to.

Peonies

This Far-Eastern design was taken from a design created around 1744 in a small German porcelain factory in Fulda. I have painted it on a round sweet-dish 16cm (6¼in) across.

Colours
Brown, cornflower blue, black, golden yellow, sea green, olive green, matt gold.

Firing
Three firings at 750–780°C (1382–1436°F).

First firing: sketch the design on to the porcelain. Outline the peonies in nasturtium red and cornflower blue, using a fine brush. Mark the rest of the design in black.

Second firing: spread out the colour on the blue petals, pushing it towards the edges with a stippler brush. The red peonies are shaded with the darker colour towards the centre. Paint the leaves in chrome green and olive green.

Third firing: accentuate some of the colours, such as the sea green, in the leaves. Paint the matt gold bands round the edge of the dish and on the base. Finally, add gold centres to the red peonies and the yellow daisies.

Quail, hedges and bamboo

Inspired by a Meissen-style design of 1710, this design has bamboo, stylised flowers and chrysanthemums sprouting from a hedge. Quail are symbols of courage and strength. The plate is 24.5cm (9¾in) in diameter.

Colours
Light red, cornflower blue, turquoise or Paris green, *café au lait* or bronze, golden yellow, 32 per cent matt gold.

Firing
Two firings at 750–780°C (1382–1436°F).

First firing: draw all the parts of this design on to the plate in red or black, using a steel-nibbed pen or a small fine brush.

Second firing: colour in the design according to the watercolour painting below. Pad a light background on the hedge (diluted red and *café au lait*). Add the gold highlights.

Yellow dragon-tiger and dahlias

These dahlia bushes with dragon-tiger and a stylised bird are in the Meissen style (a Kakiemon design from around 1735–50). On two sides of this 25cm (9¾in) four-sided vase I have painted a dahlia bush, and on the other two a dragon-tiger and a bird resembling a heron.

Colours

For the dahlias: nasturtium red, Paris green, matt gold, and a mixture of cornflower blue and grey. For the dragon-tiger: black, Paris green, cornflower blue, nasturtium red, light yellow-brown, matt gold (for the eye). For the bird: nasturtium red, black, golden yellow, lime green, sea green, light brown (for the claws and beak).

Firing

Three firings at 750–800°C (1382–1472°F).

First firing: trace the designs on to the porcelain. Draw the outlines of the dragon-tiger with the special pencil and mark them in in black with a fine brush. Shade the tree-trunk using a larger brush and cornflower blue mixed with grey. Outline the branches in blue and the dahlias in red, using a very fine brush. Paint the heron as shown in the watercolour design above.

Second firing: pad the dragon-tiger's body with light yellow-brown. Strengthen all the colours (heron, dahlias, etc.).

Third firing: with matt gold, paint a decorative band of scales around the neck of the vase and add a gold band to the base. Highlight the inside of some of the flower petals and the branches of the bush with matt gold.

Meissen-style birds

These three ideas for a round design would look good on a vase, a platter or a plate. An egg-shaped golden motif decorates the circumference of the second design.

Colours

Design 1: olive green, lemon yellow, nasturtium red, golden violet, light blue, violet of iron, sea green.

Design 2: nasturtium red, golden yellow, black (for the eye), moss green, violet of iron, matt gold (for the frieze).

Design 3: turquoise, violet of iron, olive green, golden yellow, nasturtium red, golden violet, light blue.

Firing

Two firings at 780–800°C (1436–1472°F) for designs 1 and 3 and at 750–780°C (1382–1436°F) for design 2.

First firing: sketch the birds with a medium-sized brush and lay down the colour in places, evening it out with a stippler brush.

Second firing: touch up the colour and bring out the detail of the feathers with a fine brush.

1. Bird with butterflies.

2. Bird and golden frieze.

3. Bird in flight.

80

Indian flowers

This design was inspired by the Meissen style around 1735. The plate is 25.5cm (10in) in diameter.

Colours

Light red, golden violet, lilac, black, yellow, violet of iron, a mixture of brown and dark pink, a mixture of moss green and sea green, 32 per cent matt gold.

Firing

Three firings at 750–780°C (1382–1436°F).

First firing: draw the design on to the plate. Outline all the flowers in light red as shown below, using a pen or a fine brush. With a medium-sized brush, paint the leaves with a mixture of moss green and sea green, and the branches with a mixture of brown and dark pink. Outline the bird in light red and mark the plumage and beak with a brush, then add a delicate border with a pen, plus a fine line with a small brush.

Second firing: fill in the various flowers with diluted colour and shade the leaves with violet of iron with a touch of green. Touch up the bird and paint a matt-gold edging round the plate.

Third firing: accentuate the colours on the flowers and the bird and touch up the gold.

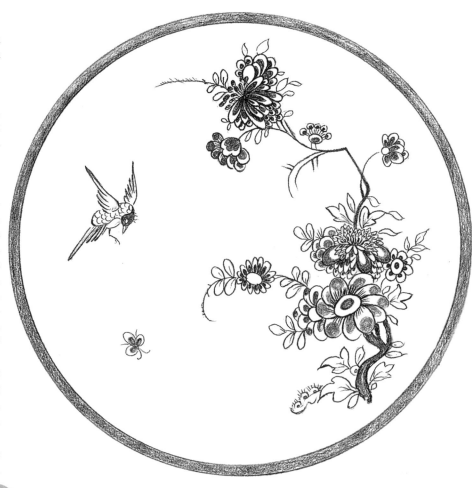

Flowery branch

I have painted these Meissen-style Indian flowers on a tea caddy 13.5cm (5¼in) high.

Colours
Nasturtium red, cornflower blue, black for outlining, chrome sea green, fir-tree green, ivy green, light rose pink, dark pink, brown, bronze, yellow, matt gold.

Firing
Three firings at 750–780°C (1382–1436°F).

First firing: draw the motif on to the porcelain and then outline the foliage and some of the flowers with black – soften this by adding a little dark blue or dark pink. Outline the flowers that will be nasturtium red and dark pink in their respective colours. On the sides of the caddy, carefully draw cross-shaped motifs with special pencil and then paint them in gold and nasturtium red.

Second firing: colour in the motifs. Paint gold bands, then paint the edges of the caddy in gold. Fill in the knob on the lid completely with matt gold.

Third firing: accentuate all the colours of the design, especially the red, pink and yellow flowers. Touch up the gold.

Butterfly and Indian flowers

Here is a Meissen-style design which you can paint on a vase.

Colours

Dark brown, light red, light blue, cornflower blue, olive green, Paris green, lilac, golden violet, golden yellow.

Firing

Three firings at 750–780°C (1382–1436°F). This is done in the same way as the *Indian Flowers* tea caddy.

First firing: outline the design in dark brown and light red.

Second firing: fill in the flowers and leaves with the relevant colours as shown.

Third firing: touch up the design.

Note: I have painted this butterfly motif on the neck of the large square vase on page 71.

Stylised flowers

This tea caddy (15.5cm (6in) high) with its Far-Eastern-style design of stylised flowers (from Fribourg, Switzerland, around 1775), is painted in yellow-brown monochrome. Its borders are decorated with a continuous frieze and two moulded leaves picked out in gold and colour. The frieze, made up of a criss-cross design with a golden dot in the centre surrounded by four coloured dots, will need to be painted very carefully.

Colours
Yellow-brown, brown with a minute touch of dark brown, matt gold.

Firing
Three or four firings at 800°C (1472°F).

First firing: sketch the design with yellow-brown. Pick out the details with a mixture of brown and dark brown using a fine brush.

Second firing: go over the details again on the flowers and leaves, using dark brown and a small pointed brush. Paint the golden frieze on the sides of the caddy, as shown above.

Third firing: carry on adding details in gold, finish the gold edging and paint a band round the base of the caddy and its lid.

Fourth firing: you will only need this if you have to touch up the gold.

Geometric motifs and golden frieze

In brown and gold, with a golden frieze on a maize-coloured background, this Ming-style design is inspired by geometry. Varieties of porcelain were created when the Chinese copied motifs sent from Europe for the East India Company, such as the scalloped designs from Rouen. I have interpreted this cache-pot, which could also be used as a vase, in an original manner. It is 21cm (8¼in) high and 20.5cm (8in) in diameter.

Colours
Dark brown, bronze, 32 per cent matt gold.

Firing
Five firings at 800°C (1472°F). With this design, you will have to be careful to keep the pattern even and symmetrical.

First firing: divide the shoulder of the cache-pot into eight equal parts. Trace on the design at regular intervals and go over it with dark brown and a fine brush. Allow to dry, and add diluted dark brown to parts of the design, evening it out by patting it with a small stippler brush.

Second firing: go over all the dark-brown parts of the design again to even out the colour and darken the background. Add little touches of bronze to other parts of the design.

Third firing: with the same bronze, highlight part of the inside of the motifs, using a medium-sized brush. Spread out and stipple with a foam pad a background on the border of the cache-pot, which is in low relief.

Fourth firing: divide the bronze band on the relief border into eight equal parts and draw on a decoration (see above) which you will then paint in matt gold. Using a turntable, paint the broad bands of gold on the rim and base of the cache-pot, and also the fine lines edging the bronze band. Add a line of dark brown to the foot of the cache-pot. Then highlight the design with points of gold.

Fifth firing: touch up the gold.

Polychromatic design on a nasturtium-red background

The design on this 18.5cm (7¼in) square ashtray is in the Graviata style and belongs to the Chinese *famille rose*.

Colours
Nasturtium red, blue-green, cornflower blue, black, rose pink, yellow, olive green, matt gold, and iridescent lustre.

Firing
Three or four firings at 750–780°C (1382–1436°F).

First firing: draw the symmetrical design inside the ashtray with a pen and outline it in cornflower blue. Paint the four butterflies on the sides of the ashtray in black, using a fine brush.

Second firing: cover the design with masking fluid and pad on a nasturtium-red background. Let the background dry thoroughly before removing the masking fluid. Now paint the motifs using diluted colour and a fine brush. Put lustre on the butterflies' wings.

Third firing: paint the butterflies' wings with diluted rose pink, yellow and light blue-green. Accentuate the colours of the design inside the ashtray – the foliage and flowers. Add a medium band of gold to frame the red background inside the ashtray and a wider one on the edge of the lip.

Fourth firing: you may have to do a fourth firing if any gold needs touching up.

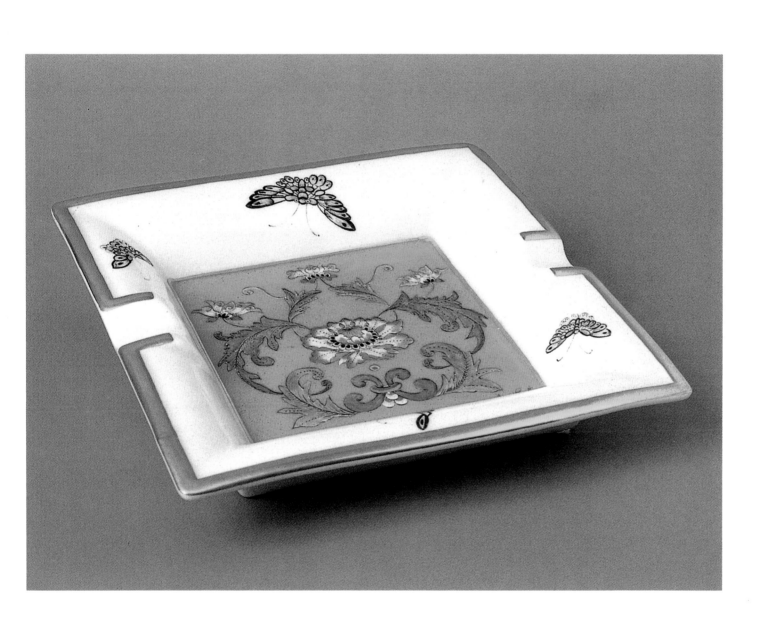

Glossary

Agate burnishing: polishing matt gold (burnishing gold) with a tool with an agate point. Agate is a silicaceous semi-precious stone.

Brushing or padding: evening out a colour by patting it with a foam pad or a special stippler brush.

Drawing: fine outline of a design done with a steel-nibbed pen.

Fibreglass brush: a special fibreglass brush for burnishing gold.

Fine drawing: the colour is prepared with sugar and water and will appear in relief. It does not need a first firing.

Frieze: a border decorated by a repeated motif painted all round an object.

Gold: a liquid precious metal which looks black. It becomes matt after firing (24 to 32 per cent fine gold) and you should then polish it. Bright gold, which has a low gold content (12 per cent), shines after firing.

Gold highlights: brush strokes of gold.

Gold thinner: this will dilute gold which has become too thick.

Kaolin: white clay used to make porcelain paste.

Manganese violet (outline violet): to make this, mix violet of iron (red of iron), dark pink and dark brown.

Masking fluid: a special red or blue substance used to protect a part of a design which is to stay white.

Medium: a ready-made mixture of fat oil and other oils, replacing the traditional preparation.

Muffle kiln: a kiln used for soft-firing on-glaze decorations on porcelain.

Polishing: polishing gold with special fine sand or a fibreglass brush.

Polychromatic: a design in several colours.

Pouncing: repeating a motif (see *Techniques*).

Relief white: powder to make a thick paste to apply to the porcelain, to make a relief design.

Sketching: applying a design in its first stage, with the details still to be added at a later stage.

Soft firing: applying a design to a glazed surface.

Special pencil: a lithographic pencil for drawing on porcelain. The line it makes disappears in firing.

Threading: painting fine lines or bands on the porcelain with the aid of a turntable.

Value: (light, medium, dark): with any colour, you can get three 'values':

> light: one coat of colour
>
> medium: two coats of colour (intermediate firing)
>
> dark: three coats of colour (intermediate firings)

White spirit: this is used to degrease porcelain and clean it before you draw and paint on it. You can also use it to clean brushes used for gold and lustre. It is a mineral solvent somewhere between petrol and paraffin and has replaced turpentine as a paint-thinner.

Wing: the flat rim of a plate or bowl.

Index

OTHER BOOKS PUBLISHED BY SEARCH PRESS

Painting China
Phyllis Imhof

Discover how to transform plain white china into exquisite hand-painted china with this delightful, informative book.

Polly Pinder's Papercrafts Book
Polly Pinder

This is another original book by Polly Pinder (author of *Polly Pinder's Party Cakes* and *Herbs in Pots*). There are simple line drawings and full-colour illustrations for a number of interesting paper projects such as windmills, simple origami models, mobiles, gift wrap and tags, and puppets and dolls. Polly delights in the use of old wallpaper samples, magazine cuttings, chocolate boxes and other disposables for these unique creations.

Paper into Pots and other fun objects: using hand-made recycled paper and papier mâché techniques
Gerry Copp

Gerry Copp uses waste paper to make papier-mâché objects and printer's offcuts to decorate them: the richly coloured bowls, clocks, mirrors, and collages illustrated show to what good effect. She shows how to recycle paper into a colourful selection of papers, then how to tear and collage them to decorate a papier-mâché base.

Decorating Eggs in the Style of Fabergé
by Pamela Purves

Using the fantastic Fabergé eggs for inspiration, the book shows how the simple egg can be transformed into a range of beautiful items, from Christmas tree decorations, christening gifts, flowers, and clocks, to jewel boxes and photograph albums. The easy-to-follow instructions will guide the reader through the many different techniques and projects.

Painted Eggs
by Heidi Haupt-Battaglia

There are many ideas for painting and dyeing eggs: using natural and chemical dyes with engraving; painting flowers and landscapes in watercolours and gouache; drawing with pencils, felt-tip pens, inks and chalk, and using batik and stencilling methods.

Marbling on Paper Using Oil Paints
Anne Chambers

Marbling goes back as far as the twelfth century in Japan. It is still popular today, and Anne Chambers' book shows how to create original papers. There are step-by-step photographs and clear instructions for the technique, followed by illustrations for effects such as marble cut, patterned, and combed.

The Art of Painting on Silk
Volumes one, two, three and four
edited by Pam Dawson

If you are looking for an exciting hobby, then try painting on silk. The combination of brilliant paints and the luxuriousness of smooth, rich fabrics creates stunning and intriguing effects. This series of beautifully illustrated books covers a range of subjects: Volume One, an introduction to silk painting; Volume Two, soft furnishings; Volume Three, fashion; and Volume Four, a pot pourri of original gift ideas.

The Art of Annemieke Mein: wildlife artist in textiles
Annemieke Mein

Annemieke's innovative and stunning textile studies of flora and fauna are beautifully illustrated in full colour in this book. Using various methods of embroidery, plus dyeing, quilting, pleating, felting and fabric-painting techniques, and all kinds of textiles, she demonstrates how to combine these skills to create an exciting sculptural medium.

If you are interested in the above books or any other of the art and craft titles published by Search Press, please send for a free colour catalogue to:

Search Press Ltd, Dept. B, Wellwood, North Farm Road,
Tunbridge Wells, Kent TN2 3DR, England

or (if resident in the USA) to:
Arthur Schwartz & Co., Inc, 234 Meads Mountain Road,
Woodstock, NY 12498
Tel: (914) 679 4024   Fax: (914) 679 4093
Orders, toll-free: 800 669 9080